Dedicated To:

Amanda Julia (Cecca) Cremone.

My daughter who "always" stands behind and supports me.
She is my "Happy Thought" and without her guidance I would go way astray.

David Tick.

Is a good friend who has always enthusiastically encouraged me to continue with
every project and without his support over the decades this book would not
have been written. Thank You.

A Special Thanks to:

RPM Fitness, Ocean Side Pilates, The Yoga Lounge, The Winthrop Book Depot and Kitaro.

Georgeane Tacelli Coleman ("Kaka Guru")
Lisa Guarnera Mignosa, Warrior Goddess!
Kathleen Duffy, Gentle Soul!
Suzanne Smith, Twisted Sister!
Laureen Sava, Intensity and Perfection!

Suzanne Martucci. A sweetheart!
Suzanne Murray- "Free " Spirit!
Victoria Valentine-Many, many thanks!

Michael and Cal, I left at the watering hole to explore the desert.

All of my friends from Byron Corner, Trav, Tass, Teli, Gibby, Dickie, Harry, Puer, Travers, Anna, Frankie S, Ronnie S, Peter G.

Nancy, Joanne, Lorna S, Linda R. Maria E, Lorna H, Bobby K, Ronnie O, Mumbles, Mickey F, of course Joe T. Carlos Variety, Stevie, Pam, Sammy & Carmela, Paul C, Bobby C, Timmy O, Paul Trav, Joe Trav, Michael Trav, Al Trav, St Dominic Savio, Andrew P., Adele L, Rufus, Jimmy M, Bobby Im, Kojak, John N, Dommy Da, George S, Horsehead, George L., Martha, Butch B, Vinny, Judy B, Tommy B , Sookie, Denise P, Brenda H, Brenda N., Lynne G, Tommy D, Tony G, Ellen T, Morgsie, Gramps, Mike C, Greg G, Leo M, Stevie Sh, The "Club" and The "Apartment" I love you all!

Jose Barbosa, kindest most generous person I know, thank you for all of those coffees, lunches, nights out and helping with the wedding, etc. You are the best!!!
John Hagan thanks for almost being a "nice guy!"
Jason Maiorano aka my "work son" thank you for the early years, the bitter middle, and reconciliation.

My family-I'm nothing without them!

OM Shanti

Preface

"Byron Corner-crosswalks and crossroads" is a collection of poems, thoughts and photographs collected over the past 50 or so years. It's that part of my being that I'm leaving behind. This is who I am when I'm alone, which is most of the time. Time spent with my best friend, myself. Other works, of fiction, that I have penned are special, nice and it is important to me that they are liked and appreciated. This work is my soul exposed. I read it and re-read it, smile, laugh and cry. It is the most important work of literature in my life. Although I hope you like, enjoy, and can feel my heart, my passion, my raison d'etre, it is ok if you dislike or disagree with it. It is important to me that you read it! I am the photographer behind the majority of the photographs. The many selfies were taken with a 35 mm camera (Fujica ST-701) with mirrors and a timer.

I spent my teenage years on the corners of Byron and Bennington Streets in East Boston. At the four corners stood Carlos Variety, Byron Pharmacy, my alma mater St Dominic Savio High School, a house with an accommodating set of brick stairs as you waited for the bus. These four corners all make an appearance in the appendix of this book. It was a time of lifelong friendships, learning, socializing, sports, music, and just having fun. The corners were always bustling with youths looking for a place to hang out or meet. There were good kids, bad kids and a lot of junkies, who were not bad people, but had lost their way. I grew up here and many of my photos and poems reflect this era. Some of the analogies may appear a bit dated. That's what time does. Enter with an open mind and you will exit with a smile.

Thank You,
Peace & Namaste

Contents

poetically unconscious

tearing from god

return

Photographs

Photographs continued (1)

Photographs Continued (2)

Appendix
A Few Photographs.

Welcome!

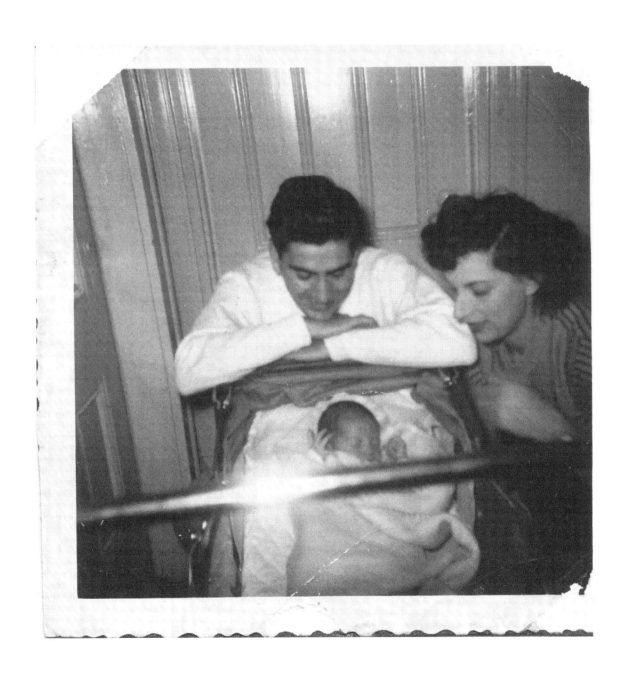

poetically unconscious

CONTENTS

3

Stranger,

Before you,
Naked,
I stand,
With truth of my being,
My essence exposed,
Fragile and vulnerable,
Like an innocent lover,
Be gentle

Fine Tuning

Gnawing at my face,
Ripping raw winter sea breeze,
Time,
That incompetent sculptor,
Etching new images with every beat.
Gravity pulling,
The fillings from my mouth,
Knocking me back into my pillow,
Facing another day.
Life,
Is so easy,
On TV.

Holidays,

A time-out
From work,
That carnivorous warlike institution,
That sucks,
The love from man,
To indulge in ones pleasures.
A time to guard
Against another man's insanity.
And OH!
OH! Too often!
A joyous time,
When aspiring resumes
Transubstantiate into obituaries.
Survival is no accident
On Holidays.

Treasure,

High School
Has been buried,
Keener than
Pirates booty,
Concealed,
Under dusty lost lazy memories,
Waiting to be rediscovered,
Uncovered,
By an old friend,
Or song,
That has recorded
Time in perpetuity,
Jolting images from sleepy cavern walls,
Shivering the soul,
About time's passage,
And getting old.

Time

This is the only moment,
The past is defined,
Future is speculative,
Now is all we have.
CARPE DIEM!

Time,
Moves with quasar-like speed.
Drop an anchor,
Or a buoy,
Let civilization
Know you were here.

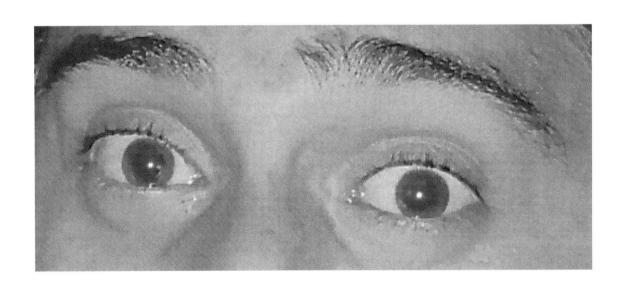

Today,

Putting down the pen,
Closing your thoughts,
For a draught of beer,
Fear,
Corporeal pleasure,
Closes the day,
One less,
Nothing gained.

Day to day
It's so easy
Not thinking.
Get your mind straight!
Know thy fate!

Daydreaming

The mind scans
Better than radar,
More efficiently than a computer,
With emotions,
Reality.
A white sail,
Contrasted by a pastel blue sky,
An angry green sea,
Catches the eye,
The mind,
Daydreaming,
Glides across open waters,
Thoughts drifting from reality,
Towards dreams,
True limbo,
Worlds of haves and nots,
Just subway stops apart,
Melting together like grilled cheese
Is today.
Dreams,
Do transcend,
When its time comes
Reality slips in like the fog.
Reality comes unrehearsed.

Temper

From the calmest sea
Ugly aggression surfaces,
Incarnate Moby Dick,
In all of its primitive fury and horror.
Spouting human acids
On flowers and lambs,
Administering irreparable psychological destruction,
Implanting cancerous cankerous memories.

The quieting calm.
The greatest pain.

Dust Dances,

In the sun light,
Through the panes of
The locked portal,
With tired blood,
On the timeworn scene,
Yawning,
That stale fading dream,
Waiting for tomorrow.

The shade drawn!
Opaque,
Coal black,
Starless,
Moonless void.

Collapsing,
Deeper into the mine,
Submerging deeper into the soul,
A black hole's gravity
Less than the forces
Trapping the spirit.

No light escaping,
No thoughts elevating,
From the dark side of the mood.

LOST

All my friends
Left behind
I miss you.

The shuttlecraft life
Has taken you
Light years
From my memory
Heart and soul.

The feel
Of your vibrant lives,
Your influences,
Shaped and molded
My personality.
I am what we were.

My friends,
Sadly,
I don't even remember
Who you were.
Intimate moments
Lost in life's daily routines.

We must meet again
And see what time
Has written.

Today,
"Johnny Tremain:,
Came home.

AMARANTHINE EYES,

Hauntingly staring from your eternal pose.
Whispering your timeless history.
Mesmerizing mortality.
Transfixed by the aura of your life force,
Captures the essence,
And the spirit we share.
Scents of yesterday
Taste like today.

Infinity,
An age,
A moment.
Recorded in a snap!
Flash! Time
Frozen!

Amaranthine Eyes
In times fraction
All dreams seemed to lie ahead,
Future penned
In fools disappearing ink.

Amaranthine Eyes
Where have you gone?

BLINDED

A beginning is just that.
It doesn't matter
Where you're at.

However,
Golden is the life
That slides into
That glass slipper.
Reality is the strife,
That grinds into
Workingmen shoes' glitter.

Don't be blinded
By your fate.
Life can be good.
It can be great.
If you keep your dreams
In front of you.

You've heard it all before,
Walls, bridges, rudely slammed doors!
They slap your face,
Suck your grace,
Knocking you back
To your lonely, lowly place.
Cut to your knees
Logic says "Please Pray!"
Or you'll pay
On your back.

but remember.
Day Dream, Night Dream
Boys Scream, Girls Scream,
"Let me out of here!"
Hear, yourself,
By not altering,
Faltering in your plans.
Keep your head,
Keep your plan on the move,
Be wise
Add chapters
Revises!
But always
"Keep your dream in front of you."

BASEBALL CARDS,

Scattered across my desk,
Lost pieces of youth,
Make me feel young again.

Rejuvenated!
Excited like a child,
Blood hammering my temples,
Opening a new pack of Baseball Cards,
Smashed in the face,
By that immortal aroma,
White residue embodying
That pink stick of happiness.
Streaking like a meteor,
My mind,
Warping through time and space,
Mining those memories,
Crashing on youthful years.
I sit motionless,
And just grin.

End Game

Hands, coordination, matching magicians.
Having vision hawks dream of .
Tiger's thighs, legs, speed, grace.
Lionized strength.
Bodies of perfection!
Images of gods!
Values of prostitutes.
Expensive cuts cheaply served.
Pride but a HA! HA! HA!
CHA-CHING!!!
The game has ended.

The Final Note

The final note's bittersweet resonance,
Slowly rose to its' celestial crescendo,
Sprinkling stardust like spent fireworks,
On its' gentle descent,
Stoking the brilliance,
Quenching the flame,
Quietly closing the curtain,
A star that burned to briefly.

The corporeal tapestry completed,
Romancer of the sweet passionate voice,
Dangles naked, unguarded and defined.
Time slowly tarnishing fame to trivia.

When idols fall,
Tumble from immortality,
Crashing through your emotions.
When all joy and pleasure,
Momentarily,
Flows to sadness and loss,
Chilling the spirit.
Fragile, frail and hurt,
Mortality,
Peeks into the mirror,
Winks at the soul,
Seeing its' place,
After the material has faded.

DREAMER,

Frustrated star traveler,
Trapped in a world,
Smaller than thee,
Unable to fly,
Get free.
Only dreams take you afar,
Away

SOUL SYMPHONY

The air guitar player
Caught every note
In a virtuoso karaoke performance.

"TEN YEARS AFTER'
Thirty years later.
"Fifty Thousand Miles Beneath My Brain."
Fifty years old. Not
missing a beat.

The reflection had changed
But the shadow remained the same.

Summer Say

The beach lay barren like tundra,
As the summer wind whipped,
Rain soaked sand,
Like punishing evil insects,
Into the faces of the few,
Who pleasurably walked,
Across nature's other side,
Just as beautiful.
As nine-to-fivers,
Drugged puppets,
Delightfully dancing to doom.
In Tube-City.
Worshipping weathermen like Pagans,
From station to station,
Praying that Sunday
be just that!
"They might as well be dead!"
Is what the man said,
"When the rain comes."

IN MEMORIAM,

To temples cracked,
Crushed under pestles
Of violence.
Victims of the day.
Vanish like dreams.
Sudden, sudden, so sudden ending.
No final good-bye,
No last kiss.
"I love you", lost in the dripping madness,
Oozing to the gutter.
The husband, wife, child, mother, father or friends,
Vacant from these eyes for eternity.
The Victims!
The Victims!
The victims of violence.
Sprawled on a cold damp lonely cement sidewalk,
Life's last breath clogged
In bloods metallic flavor,
Whispering eyes of sympathetic onlookers
Thanking God it wasn't them.
A rumbling ambulance
Sirenning to a Save Center.
Strange faces of body mechanics,
Whose love belongs elsewhere,
The last worldly contact.
All too much like a dream.
All too real.
To those
Who had nothing say
To madness and insanity,
Not quite martyrs,
Just victims,
Sad it is to say
There are no answers
Today.

To CGJ

Deep Down
Beneath the cranium cradle.
Surrealistic silent films,
Continuously play
Screaming for private screenings!

The unconscious speaks
In powerful understated undertones,
Under sheets and pillows.
Communicating with discriminating audiences
With acute subliminal hearing,
Revealing mysteries as facts,
In imagery
And symbolic treks.

MUSIC

With long face,
Down,
Depressed,
Nailed to yourself,
Like an overpowering drug,
Or Jesus,
Chin scrapping pavement,
Wrong side of the bed syndrome,
Excessive Vonnetgutian gravity,
An overworked Atlas,
A melancholic Hamlet.

Ah! Music!
Raises you like a Phoenix,
Day after day.

ROCK AND ROLL

Mirror of truth.
Mirror of time.
Rock me to my meaning.
Incubate my soul.
Nurse my undying child,
That last link to purity.
Strip the lacquers from my grain.
Expose the truth!
Let me feel pain,
So pleasure may arise,
From under layers of delusions,
Illusions from a sleeping society,
Bent on superficiality
And plastic.
Who am I?
Simple, but whom?

PRESSED,

By unfriendly sheets of cotton.
Restless,
As a baby in wet diapers.
Yesterday's news
Ticket tapering across my mind
As though it should have historical significance.
Problems magnified.
A cacophonous symphony of sounds,
Orchestrated by silence:
A showers distant drip
Thundering my name.
Rattling radiators
Evil hissing,
Incessant clock ticking,
Stealing time.
Rhythmic breathing
Of the warm machine besides me.
Swishing sounds of cars
Forcibly breaking air.
Slamming car doors and voices
Blindfolded by the hour,
Find their way.

Ideas remembered.
Ideas lost.
An endless parade of dead
Marching up my stairs.
Subconscious masochism
Playing head games
Suppressing sleep!

ERUPTIONS,

From the heart and soul,
"Tis the Poets' art
and goal…

Poetry,
Just a word,
Like all bound by Webster,
Is not a science.
Rather,
Unconscious acts of defiance.
Translating images from cerebrum deep,
Holding thoughts hard to keep,
Illuminating all of our worth
With pen in flow,
Touching on grounds,
Never touched before,
Through natures window,
Deep within the soul,
In search of truth…

tearing from god

CONTENTS

53

Black Beads,

Serpentinely coiled round
My bedpost,
Have I forsaken Thee?
You,
Dangling under INRI,
Have whispered many
Sweet dreams.
Good friend,
I never looked you in the eye.
My thoughts were at your ear.
I've fantasied in your presence.
Did I offend Thee?

Some say you limply hang
From your hooks
Like a pig in a butcher shop.
Not I,
For you are much to thin,
Your emaciated frame
Drapes with humility.
Time has done nothing
To change this.

You poor Christ!
Slayed by an infinity of pens,
Defamed by many,
Yet your humanity remains.

Of GOD (a thought)

I want to believe in you,
But,
What of Satan,
Your right hand man?
What did he see
That was not perfect?
I want to go to heaven,
But,
If Satan rules over Hell,
Then shouldn't he be an Ally
To all that enter?
Why would he hurt his followers?
Is he hurting God
By taking one of his beings?
But,
Who made Satan and why?
The Gods are out of control,
On patrol,
For a new beginning,
Paradise found
Awaits a new
Pair of genes.

OCT 71

57

Insanity,

Is peaking!
Pure thoughts and feelings,
Camouflaged in a confused
Complex conscious mask.
The mind
Perplexed by infinity,
Pre-occupied with perception,
Meandering in a chaotic-flux,
Marking individuality,
Held together by education!
All good is learned
All that is not,
Comes with a poor product
Crafted by a disorganized
Embarrassing God!

The Road,

Taken
Down a dark dismal
Seductive industrial path,
Glutted with dazed, defeated.
Dead-fallen aspiring dreams,
Snared by the economic juggernaut.
Detours, chameleon impermanent survival,
Time, momentum, gravity, accelerating irreversibility,
Makes its' prisoner,
Wanting to cry,
Killing the spirit,
Survival!
Brainwashed!
Fouled!

Ode to 45 (Where have the Muses gone?)

Melodious, joyous symphony of spring
Has faded into oblivion.
Inaudible,
Impenetrable, deaf, dead, spirit.
Calloused, dulled synapses,
Experience stealthily slaying innocence.
OH!
Those annoying sounds and rhythms of nature
Distracting concentration!
"Life's Star eclipsed by
False choices and necessity!
"Child is the father of man."
In the process
The transition,
The growth,
Something went amiss.
Think of this?
Child is the father of death!
Yet,
In youth
All seemed possible.
Beauty was abundant
We were untethered-boundless.
Today
Muted by survival,
Beauty is a sad detached,
Obscured memory.

63

Compliance 101 (the follower)

Life under an ubiquitous cloud,
Diminished by its omnipresent shadow,
Defected demagnetized compass,
Genetically programmed to acquiescence,
Waiting for a command.
Good Boy!
Sheep!
Damned!
Unable to break free!

You seduce me in my dreams
With pleasure scenes.
What are your secrets?
If I listen to you,
Then,
What of me?
If I follow?
Who will lead.

Strapped to a wheelchair
Inside a paralytic brain
Fading into insanity.
Dissolving into nothingness.

Molten Chaos

Forgotten more than I know,
High School, College,
Before and after
Blurred,
Broken windshield wiper disaster.

In retrospect, untold good times
I suspect,
Many bad times
Took place,
Lost in synaptic space.

What does it mean?
Anxiety about the future,
Getting older,
Slowly accelerating along
Life's muddled grain conveyor,
Over it's peak-"Coming down fast
Helter Skelter" it goes on.

It's all so confusing!
The thought of God and War!
All the misery we endure!

Humanity-Insanity!
The World is Molten Chaos!
Checkout is soon enough,
But,
I like music.

The Creative Mind,

Solves social situations.
Unable to understand
Wall Street
Sesame Street disparities,
Subtle life tragedies,
Top to bottom
Winter to Autumn,
Siamese in nature,
Time creeps,
Memories daze,
Subway trains screech,
A child reaches for affection
The primary leads to an election
Another commander and chief
With questionable beliefs
Losing control
Of our system
Let alone our souls!

Ocean Sand Mind

Drifting, ocean sand mind,
Thought to thought,
Emotion to emotion,
Thought to emotion,
Not grasping the meaning.
So confused,
Grabbing at clouds,
Sifting through your
Hands of time,
So sad.
Long ago I was a poet,
Of sorts,
Hearing the echoes,
Forefathers, predecessors,
Friends, relatives,
Singing songs
Of experience.
So depressed!
Time a temporary companion
With no loyalty
Takes then abandons.
I am the Tyger
I was the Lamb,
In my innocence,
Ignorance was bliss.
Now-all of this!
Is life,
For me
For you
One and one
Is not
Really two.

"Up The A"

The fresh clean country air
And dust
Slowly turned to snot,
Sometimes people
And things
Seem what they are not.
Deceived and fooled
Not seeing the grunge
Only their reflection
At the bottom of the bowl.
Shallow,
Not their fault
Conditioned
Cosmetic lot.
Worshipping Network Lords,
Tubes and chips.
Bled by doctors,
Claimed by insurance,
Bankers keep our interest,
We smile ☺
Taxes,
Sam says thanks,
To you and nature,
For having
Anus-Biggest,
No this "ain't" no Biblical Place
Only
Sodomy Somora!

Vacation,

A recess from reality.
A moment for dreams.
A time to relax,
Your body and mind.
A moment of,
Inflated superficial importance.
Vaunted, vaulted jolts of ambition.
Whispering success fueled by
Slushy Pina Coladas
Frosty draught beers
Strobing, surrealistic, self images
Flashing like a needy drug.
The body bakes in nature's oven.
Imagining the melting of fleshy fats
And imperfections.
Adonis we are,
Wasting away in the sand
Nature's surf messaging your feet.
Ah! Vacation
Shangri-La,
A time too short
For most.

So,

To be human,
Is to cry,
To be human,
Is to die

Blue or Pink

Today,
The sparkle dazzles,
Glimmers in the eye,
Reflects back to you.
Clandestinely transforming
Tomorrow,
Snailing along,
Your father filters through.
Summer blizzards cools the passion,
Serendipity,
Surreptitiously settles into Grandpa's slippers.

A cancer stricken octogenarian
Feebly cries, "Ma! Mama! Pa! Papa!"
From his morphine cloud,
Skipping over
Like and old overplayed record,
All that' in between.
Oasis dot the desert.
We move on,
We move on.

October 9th 1984

Autumn falls again,
Tumbles, tripped child,
Dirtying its' pristine hands.

Peace and Love
Meaningful words,
Lost in the aborted flight
Of the dove.
Shot down game bird?
In a preserved land

A strange land of liberty and freedom.
A land of violins and guitars.
A land of villains and heroes.
A land where villains are heroes
A land where heroes are villains.
A land of paranoia and schizophrenia.
A land of dreams and nightmares.
A land with a dreadful dichotomic Soul!

81

Future Roads

"She loves you, Yeah! Yeah Yeah!"
Screaming, crying with joy.
Music rained from heaven,
Replenishing starved minds,
Paving future roads.

"Give Peace a Chance."
Grieving, sorrowful, painful weeping.
Messages of love
Drowned in howling gunfire.
Paving future roads.

Dead at Forty.
Flesh,
Reduced to Ashes.
Flesh,
Reduced to a memory.
Paving future Roads.

Christmas 1980

12-25-1981

This was the first,
This was the saddest,
This was Christmas.

A day is a day,
A dollar is a dollar.
We're not fooled.

Consciousness is a drug.
Underneath
Nana is Dead!
Farewell.

Nana

Journeying into the future,
It's only the past that matters,
Memories trapped in a maze
Foggy dulled and hazed.
In a complex Guernican scene.

A blank page
Resurrects like magic
Especially when thoughts
Turn dark and tragic

Making mistakes,
Define our moments,
Causing permanent pain
Perpetual torments
The price for not
Being God.

I've been down
Below the conscious
Since you're not around,
So very blue and empty
Without you,
All I have to do,
Is get a signal,
Subtle worldly reminder,
To stop and think,
Sweet memories that you evoke,
When your image and philosophies,
Dance through my thoughts,
A shadow from a moving car
On a sunny day.
Memories buried to the soul,
A day, just another song sung.
A buried loved one.

Papa,

Was the monument old,
An assumption!
Of time (in perpetuity) and time again,
(OH! Maybe Eden)
Never getting his due.
I loved him!

Entrapped in my genes.
A prisoner of my conscience.
"SWEETA Poison," was his medicine.
"DIS IS DA Life," was his motto.
Yes, a special case,
With this thought,
One last tomorrow.

Code Blue and You

Laughter, joy and always a boy
Slaughtered, destroyed,
Like a useless broken toy
In a wink of time.

Through blurred nephewed vision,
Emanates a still life.
In animations,
Titillating, cataracts of memories,
Freeze framing pain and joy,
All to pain –don't want it to be over
(it can't be over).
Fade to black
        Enter smiling sadness:

            "Twinny Twinny
             Uncle Dear
             How I wish that
             You were here."

91

"Quiet Guy"

Barely audible background vocal.
Never heard above the crowd,
Never lost in it.
Kind gentle,
Quietly wearing his tragic shroud.

He was the one,
The one,
To get closer to.
Missed opportunity
Slipping through times fickle
Clumsy fingers.

Quietly loved
Quietly missed.

93

Silent, Silent

Silent, silent, so silent house,
Trembles not,
As darkness rules,
Invisibly roaming
From room to room,
With the softest slippers,
Blanketing dreamers.
An Ominous phone ring
Shatters silence!
Grief spreading like a plague
Suffocating awaking sleepers,
Its' ally,
Death,
Momentously as a clock tick,
Grabs ungraciously snatched,
From life's cradle.
Man mass of accumulated time,
Allowing grief
To fill the void
Left by death.
        "John, John the Pipers son
        Run so farst,
                He broke his arse,
        Never go back to Boston Mass."
                (Farewell & Thank You U. J.)

The Great One,

Was
Anti-Gravity,
Elevating the spirit,
Lifting the heart,
Washing the room in a brilliant sunrise,
Packing smiles with his wit,
Freely handing them out,
On his regal arrival,
He was,
Raconteur Supreme,
A Pied Piper of Tales.
True to his school,
Defender of his country,
Honored to serve with the men of his war.
It's time to say good-bye to:
Eddie Lambert and Joe Joseph
And hundreds of others,
I feel I knew you well.

A Mickey Mantle glove from Bucky Warren's.
Monkey faces at the Shawmut Bank,
A trip to the Franklin Park Zoo with Mary,
A photo on my desk,
A daily reminder of his undefined greatness,
Racks my emotions
Making this incomplete.

Cemetery of the Mind.

I try not to be morbid,
But,
The loss,
Sudden in a sense,
Of Debbie
So young,
Trembles and Shatters
My heart.
Reaching for one good memory
Brings tears,
The loss is so great,
Greater for others.
I needed a hug
Uncertainties of life,
Frightening and Frustrating,
All has been said
About here,
And after,
Trying to find laughter
Amidst the pain
Reliving the final days,
When time stopped.
No regrets,
I want to scream,
Hoping that this is a dream
Driving me insane
Not knowing who to blame!

P.B.F.

Friend,
We fought the same war.
Enigmatic You!
Who?
Who "were you?"
Friend,
Emotional factor maximum
Keeps me from thinking of you.
But,
I miss you.
War does funny things to us.
Your star shone with brilliance.
You did not short sell your wares.
Today,
Friend,
You're focused
In my thoughts.

Diana Princess of Broken Dreams

Viewing my world,
Glassy eyed,
Physical Stranger,
Spiritual friend,
Breaks my heart.

Nothing makes sense.
Your common death
Is astounding.

Your visage,
Your image,
Your beauty,
Your essence,
Goddess traits,
Material of
Romantic Poets.

You are so loved!

Maybe thereafter
Reveals
How it unraveled.

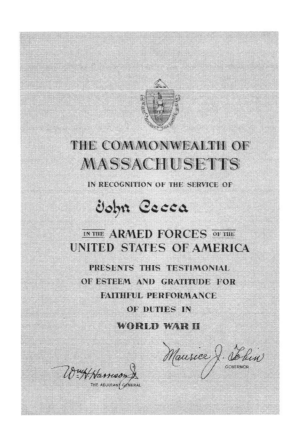

They Wait,

At home,
Crippled with fear.
They wait,
Incubating the essence
Of the shadows vacuum.
The bill is due!
What is the price of freedom?
One soldier,
One being,
A newspaper blurb.

They wait,
Powerless,
With pulsating palpitating apprehension,
For news.
An existence defined,
Into a scrapbook of tears,
Vibrant, vivacious engine of life,
Reduced to a memory.
A hero!
An honorable label,
Justifying,
The premature ascension of a soul,
For the privilege,
Freedom.

Sadly,
The price of freedom,
Is not paid for
Equally,
Most assume that it is free.

They wait at home,
Time dripping, a frozen lava lamp,
Tracing the past,
Defining love and family.
Most will walk in the sunshine,
Of their loved ones,
At least once more,
The few will travel,
The expensive, eternal.
Proud path of the horse drawn caisson.

Passing.

The sun is setting,
My eyes are closing,
Love is all around.
Did it really happen,
A dream,
So fast it all did seem.

Time, oh time,
You measured me,
Wrapped me in you history,
Gain my confidence,
Then shattered me.
　　Days of youth, days of glory
　　Passing time writes the story.

Happiness is not found in fame,
We all play life's meaningful games,
Moments of pleasure,
Encompassed by pain.

Everyone loves a hero,
Wanting a piece of you,
World of walls and disillusionment.

Time, oh time, see how you recorded me.
Wrapped me in your misery,
Gave me things,
Dreams should be.

　　Days of youth, days of glory,
　　Passing time tells the story,
　　Doesn't matter who you are
　　Even the brightest star,
　　Will fall.

So, so, long ago,
A millennia, a moment.
A beginning, an ending,
Friends closer to the heart than blood,
Distant as a galaxy.

Time, time, don't run out on me?
Just one moment to reflect,
Where fame is found in happiness.
　　Days of youth, days of glory.
　　Passing time rights the story.

return

CONTENTS

108

Photo by Georgeane Tacelli Coleman.

109

RETURN

A child with no home,
Pitiful is the Dark Side of the Mood.
The Muses have survived,
Omniscient to high-tech and concrete,
Assuaging damaged souls,
Opening the heart and ears,
Empowering the senses to alleviate fear
Enlightening dark roads and avenues
Allowing Nature and Love,
To sedate realties pang.
Even a Black Hole
Succumbs to dreams!

Children sing,
Children play,
Children laugh,
Their lives away.

The Artist,

A child lost in play,
Digging their stage,
No regard for the time
Of day.
Nothing to do with age,
There is only today,
Adrenaline pulsating from the soul,
A geyser of illumination spouting
Into a spectrum of creation.

The Cow Cried,

It sacrificed its' soul
For a Happy Meal
Or
A leather strap.

A leather strap
Finding the waist
Of a young man.

A leather strap
Finding the flesh
Of a little boy.

A Vision

A vision is
Worth a thousand years.
Simple is happiness,
Simple is greed.
Jellyfish man
Is lazy.
Selfish man
Is crazy
With power and hate,
To have more is
Love
Thy neighbor's soul
Possession
Of all of his wares,
Compound simplicity,
With endless marathons
Of insatiable riches.
Grabbing rainbows with
Slimy fingers of passion,
The purest
Tainted by osmosis.
A vision is
Worth a thousand tears.
Simple is greed,
Simple is happiness.

119

Save a Tiger,
Eat a cow,
Pig, or chicken,
Save a Leopard,
Have a piece of Veal
How ideal,
Selecting slavery and sacrifice
Over extinction.

To Live,

Let the string go
Of those
Helium filled
Fears.

The Power,

The Power, the Power,
The Power of the note,
The Power of the chord,
The Power of the failure,
Of the diplomatic accord.

> Dancing in the light.
> Moving to the music.
> Persuaded by the Power,
> The Power of the note.
> The Power of the chord.

Light years and Jungian fears,
Saving ancient tribal rites,
From the Power of the wrong.

> The Power of the lyric,
> The Power of the song,
> The failure of nations,
> They don't sing along.

Does there have to be Songs of love,
To fill day to day misery?
Can't we stop and say, "Have a nice day."
Instead the need to pray.

> The Power of the Id,
> The Power of the Ego,
> The aborted mission of
> The bald eagle.

Where do we turn for preservation,
Salvation,
Wrapped in our drugs,
Trapped in our dreams,
Societal giants smile at our screams!

> The Power of the note.
> The Power of the chord,
> What is Power?
> When the greatest Power
> Is the Power of pain?

124

Even The Small,

Can fall,
Playing the hand wrong,
Cards not falling,
Keys not turning
It's a yearning,
Burning,
Gets me to my car,
Away from this bar,
Seeing how fast
I can drive,
How high I can fly,
Striving,
For the stars.

Joe C-"The" Salesian

As a boy,
Blinded by I,
ME!
He,
Was an obstacle,
Tortuous teacher of math!
He was so old,
Puerile thought
Would have him dead,
By my time taught.
Gentle killer was he,
Only concern was me.
Beat me to grade zero,
Still my hero.
Years, decade past.
Shining in different light,
He the sun,
I a cloud.
Though no great scholar,
Earning his honor.
In heaven his lesson plan,
Is the archetype,
Of a true
Salesian.

Where has time gone?

Infinitesimal to God,
The Universe,
A lifetime, eternity
To mortality,
Chronicled in memorabilia verses,
Annals of family photos,
Scrutinizing the seed,
Flowering to fruition,
A sweet elation,
Yet selfish feelings,
Loneliness,
Failure to my soul,
Wants to revert back to childhood.

At times thinking of the things
I had
Made me rich.

Would that I could replay time,
All of its' unique sights, scents, sounds,
And all senses, relive them all!

Life moves vibrantly,
Washed by time,
Fades and frays away.

To You

An inaudible background vocal,
Barely detected star on a foggy eve,
A mouth with no tongue.
A brain-no IQ,
Length x width x height,
No dimensions.

Sudden Success,
To You

"I know him well."
An echo of Lennon,
Supernova,
Walking in God's shadow,
More ears beckon than E. F. Hutton,
Einsteinium cranium equivalent,
Working with multiple dimensional extra-terrestrials.

To you,

Standing deaf to reason,
Blinded by rationalizing religion,
Guessing your way through reality.

To You,

Blinded by the system.
Could not separate truth from illusion,
Could not separate happiness from ambition,
Cannot see your soul in the mirror!

Insanity never lay at my doorstep.

Old Friend?

I met today,
A friend from long ago.
He wasn't alone,
Neither was I.

He felt that my ears
Were more important
Than my mouth.
We drank
He talked.

It was a good time,
I think.
He talked loudly, boisterously,
Proudly boasting his accomplishments,
And his ambitions.
Wow!
It continued like a bad verbal-diarrhea.
This good time started to stink.

I tried to use my mouth,
Out came a word,
I think?
Yes one word!
Must have been a turd!
His voice could be heard,
Over mine.
Trying again-same result.
I chuckled within.
He thought it was approval.

He felt that my ears
Were more important
Than my mouth.

Texture of Time.

Pristine, pliant, modeling clay,
Framing, freezing, moments in time,
Continuous cerebral time capsule,
Consuming experience,
Imprinting, fingerprinting
Personality,
Individuality, uniqueness,
Private sanctuary,
Vaulted in a library of memories.

The senses activate,
Oscillating in temporal distorted moments.
Accessing data,
Flashing back,
Without notice,
To fixed moments,
Nebulous and obscene,
Triggering emotions.
The texture of time
Giving form, shape,
And definition.

OH XMAS TREE,

Majestic, prominently displayed
The pinnacle of religion and pride,
Symbol of the holiday
Prematurely laying in an
Early winters wake
Out with the garbage!

OH XMAS TREE,
How the mighty fall,
Gone in a whim.
Irreverently trashed!
Your job completed.

A man,
with less than a home,
ragged, torn,
a cheap alcoholic
scent of the season,
clinging to his mangy beard,
rummages through the days sales.
amongst bottles, recycles, swill and other,
without hesitation seizes the early season trophy.
he knows no god, but lives in the serpent's belly.
Today,
was a lucky one.
with a sip of wine and few crumbs of bread,
feeling blessed
that the fallen symbol had found him.
proudly placing the trophy on his mantle,
he wraps himself in his blanket.
transfixed by the icon,
slowly falling asleep,
to the rhythm of crossing vehicles.
cupping his frostbitten hands,
his breath looking like smoke,
merrily
nods towards tomorrow.

138

The Journey.

The journey,
Sparked,
Melancholically twisted time,
Spiraling into a roulette wheel panic.
Starting on my desk,
Desperately seeking a guide,
Pilotless,
The troupe engaged,
In banal trivialities,
Lost moments,
Sinking the soul.
So much wasted time.
Who thought a lark,
A photo in the dark,
Could hold such emotion.

Best Friend,

Oceans away,
Long time no hear,
The heart flutters,
With fear,
Tears.
Meetings,
Space stations apart.
Closeness.
Telepathic thoughts of love.
We must be travelling
In light years,
For 31 seems
To be 21 or 17,
When we are together.

143

Sometimes,

Friends get lost,
Tossed from today,
Like daily news,
Never forgotten,
Like the "Baltimore Catechism."

Sometimes,
Friends,
Are separated by time,
Diverging Frostian roads,
Hopefully meeting.

Sometimes,
Friends,
Circulate your thoughts,
A rhyme in need of improvement.
And forget me not,
Haunting and taunting,
That lazy side,
Making time
Its' master.

Sometimes,
Feelings are never expressed,
Suppressed
By small talk and fears,
Filtered, distilled
By time,
Clarity is framed.

Always,
Sometimes friends
Are eternal.

To Dance

Oh!
To dance
To go out
And dance,
Like a Tribal American Indian,
On the verge of extinction,
Around a blazing bomb fire,
Chanting to deaf dead gods,
Prance like a wild possessed stallion,
Into a funeral pyre,
Ascending heaven,
Cremated spirit.

Oh!
I want to dance
Rhythmically
To the music
Sensually shake
Rattle and roll,
Exposing my soul.
I really want to dance!
With a nymphonic princess,
In a club,
Intoxicated with spirits,
Laughing, having fun,
Until I come,
To my senses.

(The Yoga Lounge, Winthrop, Ma.)

Chilling

Summers' eve cool salty ocean clam- bed breath
Chilled the Chardonnay filled frame,
The Big Dipper scooped
The dulcet rhythms
Of Joni
Feeling Blue
From this 8th floor balcony.
Sipping new thoughts
Reasoning with sleep and indifference,
With ujjayi pranayama
Gentle exhalation
Mother Nature heats the core,
Thoughts tumbling in a cerebral vinyasa
Senses smiling
Enjoying the clock's tick,
Adding a note
To another invisible folder.

Caveat Emptor

A full-time poet's credits
Are substantial,
A part-time creators' merits,
Are suspect,
To additional scrutiny,
Like legal documents.
Inspiration
Doesn't knock on the door.
Lost labor,
Tribulations
Become a stigma,
"I was there."
With no bed of roses,
Paying the florist,
Dearly,
And taxes yearly.

151

1446761

Like a dragon, I exhale the vapor.
Knowing that one more draw will do.
Holding the pipe, I want more.
More! More! More until I feel like you.
Gazing, I feel as if I were omniscient.
Moving and grooving, I don't yield.
My immobility amazes me. I'm content
As if I were in the Elysian Field.
Now I see, not as you, or you,
I see me.
You think you do.
No, I'm free!
Puff, puff, puff.
Get on the stuff!

(Just a quick note that this was written during the summer of 1970. I was a freshman at the University of Massachusetts-Amherst. The original title was Sonnet 1446761?)

Sea of Future

Yesterday's dreams are fading the scene,
The future seems just as cloudy,
Moving faster than the speed of thought,
Something is wrong,
I'm frightened, so distraught

     Slow down, go back
     Find yourself, un-track
     Slow down, it's never too late
     Find yourself, don't hesitate!

In the mirror-I see my face!
Drowning in the sea of future.
Fading dreams...
Anxiety screams
"Drowning in the sea of future!"
Oh, to see the future?

Is it so hard-to slam the brakes!
Reverse direction-make that break.
It's you life. Don't be fooled!
Let future work for you.

     Slow down, go back.
     Find yourself, un-track.
     Slow down, it's not to late.
     Find yourself, don't hesitate!

Drowning in the sea of future.
Oh, to see the future.

Tomorrow comes-guaranteed.
Not for your-not for me.
Leave your mark.
Escape! From that mind dark.

Appendix

A few photographs.

161

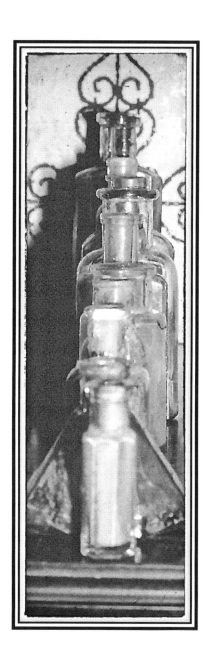

"You talking to me?

"You can't escape your demons just by leaving home." Max Cady.

Made in the USA
Middletown, DE
02 July 2019